# ST to SUCCESS

PARALLELS BETWEEN HEALING
FROM A STROKE AND FINDING YOUR
CONFIDENT SALES VOICE

# SUZYWIGSTADT
(simonson)

# STROKE TO SUCCESS
## —parallels between healing from a stroke and finding your confident sales voice

Copyright © 2017 Suzy Wigstadt

ISBN: 978-1-943157-40-2
Printed in the United States of America

Published by Master Networks Publishing
www.MasterNetworksPublishing.com

# DEDICATION

I am dedicating this book to my family.

>My family who was given to me by blood.

>My family who has chosen me in friendship and love.

>My family who has inspired me in business.

>The love of my life, who became my family the first day we met!

Without their love, support, and belief in me I wouldn't be who I am or where I am today!

Thank you for your belief, when I didn't believe in myself!!

You have changed my life!!

# INTRODUCTION

I am honored that you are taking the time to read my words. Going from having a stroke to achieving success has been an amazing journey. It has included moments that were ugly, beautiful, difficult, frustrating, exciting, and joyful! I am thankful to share with you my journey and the parallels I've learned between finding my confident voice and healing from my stroke.

I am not much of a reader and have struggled with insecurity, lack of confidence, anxiety, and depression since I can remember, so getting these words out on paper has not been easy! I know that this needs to be written, not only for you, but for myself. I have fought hard to build my confidence and have had this book running through my head for years. It is time!

Please sit back and relax while you read this. My hope is that this book will help you listen to your heart, your passion, and your gut!

You were *created exactly how you are* because our world needs *exactly who you are*. Specifically YOU! There is no one else with your fingerprints or heartbeat.

Try to picture us sitting, chatting over coffee. We're telling stories, connecting, and learning from each other. That's how I would love for you to read and enjoy this book. If something "sits well with you," please take action! That is the beautiful thing about life – we can all see, hear, and read the same thing and take away what applies to us individually.

I am so excited to let you in on how my life has gone from having a stroke to having success.

Lots of love!

     —Suzy

# CONTENTS

| | |
|---|---|
| Dedication | 3 |
| Introduction | 4 |
| Change! | 7 |
| Family Is Everything | 27 |
| Fight for What Is Yours | 45 |
| Seven to Twelve Times | 59 |
| It All Starts with a Cookie | 79 |
| Leave Your Junk at the Door | 95 |
| Listen to Your Gut | 103 |
| You Are Exactly What Your World Needs | 113 |
| Possible Action Steps | 127 |

# CHANGE!

September 25, 2010 changed my life.

When I was young, I was the girl who was constantly sick. I was small, artsy, and "happy, smiley, friendly" as my dad would tell me when I threw a tantrum. I felt everything for everyone around me. Inside I was a mixture of love, joy, peace, kindness, goodness, insecurity, fear, despair, and anxiety sprinkled with hope and trust. I was always the caretaker. I deeply felt the emotions of my family and friends and wanted to help them. I formed a habit and lifestyle of being more concerned with other people than I was for myself!!

In the months leading up to September 25, 2010, migraines were a normal part of my daily life. I wasn't in the habit of listening to my body or taking care of myself. I was getting about four hours of sleep a night and working around 100 hours a week. For 60 hours of my week, I was an account executive for a title company. Another

30 hours a week were spent as a photographer –
capturing and editing beautiful moments. I
devoted 10 hours a week to building my
photography website. I was really good at
ignoring what my body was telling me. This was
my life. This is what I knew. It was normal to me.
I accepted that I would feel that way and take
medication for the rest of my life. I loved being
needed. I was always the *Yes Girl* and put
everyone else above myself. I still haven't
mastered balance, but my *no muscles* are a lot
stronger now. I am growing daily and learning
more about myself. I am now able to say "no" if it
doesn't line up with the needs and boundaries
I've set for myself and my family.

September 25, 2010 was an abundant day. I got
my regular four hours of sleep the night before
and woke up with a migraine. I took some over-
the-counter medication to ease the pain and
went to photograph a beautiful, young family
before capturing an amazing wedding. There is
nothing like being invited to document beautiful
moments that will never be had again but will be
remembered for a lifetime. I loved all of my jobs
and thought that I could continue doing them

all. Looking back, I can see clearly that *I thought I wasn't important but what I did was.*

I had been a professional photographer for seven years. I was excited that my day was filled with love. Weddings are such beautiful, emotional, and important events. When a bride and groom decide to hire me, they automatically have a second photographer for the day. We always provided a second photographer with our packages to provide multiple angles of one moment and capture amazing candid moments. Typically, my mom and I would photograph together. I loved this because we know each other so well. We naturally know each other's strengths and weaknesses without needing to say a word to each other to fill in the gaps.

My mom and I started photographing together by accident. I went through a traumatic heartbreak when I was 21 years old. Depressed, I stayed in the house for months. My mom had taken my sister's senior pictures and was being asked to take other people's senior pictures. My brother, sister, and I grew up with her camera constantly in our faces. I tell people that if we sneezed, she got a picture of it! Also, if there wasn't a picture,

9

it didn't happen. The proof of something was always in the picture. Arguments have been either won or lost because of a picture!

Mom would say, "I feel like taking pictures today … you want to go somewhere?" The three of us would coordinate our outfits and hop in the car. We would get really cute shots, goofy shots, and always the "we're done now" shots! My mom was used to the three of us posing ourselves, so she didn't know how to tell someone else to pose and capture it. She asked me to come along. She said it was to pose people because she didn't feel comfortable doing it – I know that was true, but I now know that it was also because she saw her broken-hearted daughter stuck and wanted to do whatever she could to bring me joy. We found out very quickly that photographing together was amazing!!

So much so that we bought a second camera so we could both shoot at the same time. More and more people heard that we were photographing together, and our weekends started to get booked with senior pictures and weddings. It grew from a hobby that got me out of the house to a professional business!

My mom and I had booked September 25, 2010 for a beautiful couple. The bride was a family friend, and we had done her senior pictures. Then one of my sister's friends asked us if we were available on the same day! We had never experienced that. In seven years, none of the weddings we were invited to capture had ever landed on the same day. We never had to turn anyone down or ask someone else to be our second photographer. For the first time ever, we could be double-booked. We had a choice. Should we say no to one wedding? Or should we invite an amazing photographer to shoot with each of us and capture both weddings? We went with the second option and accepted both weddings. As an added bonus, I got to shoot with one of my best friends, who is a fantastic photographer!

As I started to photograph the bride and all of her beautiful bridesmaids, I could feel the medicine wear off, so I took more throughout the day. I was so excited for the day that I didn't eat much or drink enough water. It was incredibly hot and my allergies were bugging me. And, to top it all off, my monthly "friend" was in town.

This was a perfect storm to have a hemiplegic migraine.

I've learned that excitement and anxiety are the same to your body; it doesn't know the difference between those two stress-makers. It had been a while since I had a hemiplegic migraine, so I really thought I was permanently over them.

I was wrong!!

Imagine a tingling sensation beginning in your fingertips and your toes, but only on one side of your body. Then that feeling starts to spread up your arm to your elbow. Then it changes from the tingling to numbness, like Novocain. It feels like your hand is someone else's attached to your body. It feels puffy and cold, like after you've gone to the dentist and have drool dripping off of your lips because you can't feel it. That numb feeling spreads from your toes to your knee.

I have had migraines since I was five years old, so I know the routine. I had just captured the wedding party walk down the aisle before they took their places. I saw the bride and her dad walking down the aisle together. It was an amazingly beautiful moment. The room was filled with love and excitement. The groom couldn't wait to have her on his arm.

I felt the numbness continue to spread. I literally prayed, "Lord, not now. Please, not now. Please take this away!"

I looked up and saw my best friend doing what she does best. I knew that she would continue to capture the ceremony. So I said to myself, "I need to just rest and it will get better."

There was a door to the right of me – but I didn't want to attract any attention to myself. Right when I was about to move, one of the bridesmaids buckled her knees and quickly fainted (she was alright). Everyone's eyes turned to her, so I was able to go out the side door.

The door led to a room with a bunch of tables and chairs. After sinking into a seat, I laid my head down to rest a little and breathed deeply. I knew that the ceremony would be over soon, but so would my ability to speak and communicate. I needed to get to my sister and best friend. My sister had experience going through these with me and has had them herself, so she would know what was happening.

I went outside and walked around the church carrying my camera in my good hand (the numbness only happens to one side of my body). I found the beautiful, red arched door that we had taken pictures by earlier with the bride and groom. The door was locked. I laid on the cement stairs with my arm over my eyes to block the bright sun and waited.

When the door opened, the bride and groom were beaming! Then I saw my best friend. I looked at her, but all I could say was, "Sis-ter. Sis-ter."

She went quickly to find her. Right when my sister and her best friend saw me, they knew what was happening. My eyes filled with tears because I knew it was bad. I knew I would need sleep to get better.

I said, "Sleep."

I thought I would get better quickly and be able to get back in and photograph the reception.

Throughout the night many people came to check on me. Luckily, my best friend held down the fort with the photography. She was a champ!

There were so many crazy things about this day and how everything came together. Here are a few:

- The groom at the wedding was a doctor. He took my vitals a couple of times.
- My sister was at the wedding I photographed. She knew both brides. If she hadn't been there, no one would have known what to do or what was going on.
- My best friend was my second photographer. She is an amazing person, and her photography is some of the best that I've seen.
- My mom was photographing with an amazing friend who seamlessly captured moments that I typically would have.
- If my mom and I were photographing together, I believe she would have been in "mom mode" and would have wanted to take care of me.

It amazed me how everything worked out next to perfectly! A friend picked me up and drove me home, where I slept for two days. That was the typical recovery time. After sleeping and bathing for a couple of days, I would return to my normal "happy, smiley, friendly" self.

That hemiplegic migraine was different.

After the numbness and lack of communication, a splitting pain would always engulf my head. The pain would shoot across my head from one ear to the other like I was wearing a headband. That time wasn't just shooting pain; it felt like a saw was going back and forth cutting through my skull. There were times where I would just moan in agony because of both the physical pain and mental frustration. I knew what I wanted to say, but I wasn't able to communicate it.

When I was home for a few days going through the "getting better routine," my family would come and check on me throughout the day. They brought me food, ran baths for me, and gave me medicine. Because I had been in this situation multiple times, going to the hospital wasn't really an option. They would only do tests and say,

"She's got abnormal brain patterns." We were also in between health insurance coverage, so my family made the decision on my behalf to stay home and go through the routine.

Four days after the hemiplegic migraine started, I took a turn for the worse. My mom called a nurse who was one of the parents from her early learning center. She asked her, "How do we know if we should take Suzy in?"

She was told, "If she starts throwing up – take her in, because then she's dehydrated and you know it's serious."

I started throwing up. This was concerning because I *never throw up*. I hate it more than almost anything! I remember crawling to a blanket on the floor in my parent's living room. I laid there until they brought me to the hospital. My memories turn to a dreamlike state after that.

I can play the memories I have back in my head like a movie. I can access them at any time. Although in talking with those who were around me and lived "the reality" of the time after the hemiplegic migraine/stroke, our recollections are different. I would have glimpses into their reality, but I felt as though I was in a dream. I don't know the moment the stroke happened; I do know that I had the mindset of a newborn baby because of it. I didn't know that I wasn't fully myself, because it was all I knew at the time.

When you hear that newborns know the people who love them right away and that they recognize the sound of voices they've heard, I can tell you that it is 100% true! I haven't just seen it and experienced it with newborns but also as a 28-year-old newborn! My soul knew my family's souls! I didn't just recognize their voices, but I knew they were mine and that they were safe! Family was in and out visiting daily.

I was in the hospital for seven days. I believe I started to come back to *this reality* at day five. I'm told that the staff was going to let me go earlier because I learned to mimic the answer that would get them to leave me alone. I learned that responding with, "Suzanne Wigstadt, 10.25.81" would make them go away.

I could copy them with my voice, but it didn't connect in my brain that I was telling them who I was. I guess I was also pretty sassy once I started coming back. I needed to take some medication and didn't want to, so I pretended to go to the bathroom and threw the medication in the garbage and tried to cover it up. I don't remember this at all, but I'm told it's what I did. So even while I wasn't fully myself, I was stubborn and sassy.

My mom slept by my side every night (thank you, Mom). I don't know if words can express how much it means to me and meant to me to have a warm body, a soul and a smile next to me!! I was never alone in that hospital room. I felt their love; my soul knew their soul. Having their presence is one of the things that I believed saved my life!

I also felt like I was swimming, no drowning, in an ocean of prayers. I was told that there were thousands of people praying for me. I felt them. Physically, I could feel all of them. If you were a person who prayed for me in this time, thank you from the bottom of my heart.

Here are a few pictures of my time in the hospital. I am thankful for where I've been. I learned and grew so much, but I wouldn't wish it on anyone's family. My family is my rock. They are my world. I am here and who I am because of them!

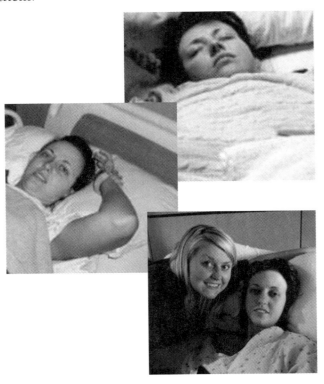

Here are a few images of when I started to feel better in the hospital. I got a bit of my sparkle back. When I started to feel better in the hospital, I knew what I wanted to say, but the connection between what I wanted and how my body would perform was disconnected. So I would smile, wink, and take pictures. I wanted to let my family know that I was there and would be back, fully.

I was released from the hospital on October 5, 2010, a full 11 days after my hemiplegic migraine. The doctors are not sure if the stroke was caused by the hemiplegic migraine or possibly a blood clot that went through the hole in my heart. No matter what the cause, I was on my road to recovery.

As I was driven home from the hospital, I remember looking at the roads that I grew up on like it was the first time seeing them. I remember walking into my parent's house; I could sense how excited and happy everyone was, but I was apprehensive. I left the only place I knew. Everything was new to me, though it felt like home at the same time.

My first memory of speaking intentionally was on October 17, 2010, a short 22 days after I had the hemiplegic migraine. My family was on the phone with my grandpa to wish him a happy birthday. Everyone was excited! I reached for the phone to join in on the celebration. I was so confident I would be able to wish him a happy birthday. I mustered up everything in me and said, "HAPPY BAPPY!"

Everyone kind of laughed. I was excited for a second but then extremely frustrated that I didn't say, "Happy Birthday." I really thought I had it down. I practiced it in my head and searched for the connection to my voice for the words, but instead "Happy Bappy" came out loud and proud. I didn't know how that moment would affect me as I began to heal.

Still today, I wish the people I know, love, and trust a "Happy Bappy!" It is something that is meaningful to me now, not just to laugh at but to remember how far my family, friends, and I have come!

Happy Bappy is a precious reminder to try … no matter how hard things are.

Pull together in yourself whatever you need to. Don't give up. Even if you feel like the delivery is not what you thought or wanted it to be, it may be exactly what you or someone else needs. Learn to laugh at the plans that don't go your way and have confidence that there is a bigger picture and a bigger purpose. You may not know when you will see it, but it's on its way. Be mindful enough to welcome it when it comes and share it when it's needed!

As the chapters of this book have been forming in my mind, I have found that there are seven parallels between healing from my stroke and finding my confident voice.

I started with the intention that this book would be best read by entrepreneurs and salespeople, because that's who I was and the parallels are between what I learned in both the healing and the earning business.

I now believe that this book is for YOU. The parallels in this book are for life, no matter where you are. In each chapter, I will be sharing stories of my life to connect with you.

Here are the parallels I've learned between healing from my stroke and finding my confident voice:

- Family Is EVERYTHING.
- Try Again, Seven Times – Twelve Times.
- Listen to Your Gut.
- You Are Number One.

- Put Yourself First.
- Fight for What Is Yours.
- There Is a Way.
- You Are EXACTLY What They Need.

# FAMILY IS EVERYTHING

I would not be telling this story if it wasn't for my family. Their presence, care, and belief in me saved my life. When I couldn't speak, they were my voice. When I tried to post things to Facebook, they were my editors. When I tried to call people at three in the morning while I still couldn't speak well, they took my phone away. One of my family members or close friends stayed with me even if they had plans.

- They were my support.
- They pushed me to be better.
- They held a healthy space for me.

As I healed from my stroke, I grew exponentially. I went from the mindset of a newborn to a two-year-old. From there, I kept growing and progressing; I had the mindset of a four-year-old, eight-year-old, sixteen-year-old, and twenty-eight-year-old before becoming as normal as normal could be. Each of my family members had a specific place in my healing.

My mom was comfort and care. She was an overwhelming place of love. She was in my bubble, exactly where I needed her! She made sure that everyone's schedule lined up so I was not alone 24 hours a day, seven days a week for three months. She made sure that I was emotionally taken care of and that I didn't feel alone.

My dad was protection and belief. He made sure that I knew I was strong and that everyone was rooting for me. He would read to me daily. I would sit with the two little lambs he bought and named for me, "Goodness" and "Mercy," one in each arm, listening to him read. I remember sitting at the kitchen table one day. He wrote 1 + 1 = on a sheet of paper and looked at me with a questioning expression on his face. I knew that I *should* understand what he was asking me, but I had nothing.

The best way that I can describe how I communicated with people was by analyzing their body language and tone of voice. I knew when someone asked me a question or when they were happy, sad, or concerned. I just wasn't able to react or respond to them. I didn't even understand the question, let alone that it was a math problem. I was always cold, so my dad bought me a heated blanket that I would bundle up in every day.

My brother was strength and humor. He would sit with me and hold my hand. I felt his strength. I felt his concern for me. I knew that there wasn't much else that mattered other than me getting better. He brought out laughter. He lightened the mood. I remember sitting on the couch with my brother, watching a Twins' game; we had our Homer Hankies out rooting for the Minnesota Twins!

My sister was confidence and my soft place to land. She did things that she normally wouldn't do, like give me a hand massage. She knew it was something that I loved and needed. She brought me back to the softy that I am. I remember our first time shopping together. When we got home, I said something sassy. She looked at me with tear streaming down her face and said, "My sister is back." I'm pretty sure we ugly cried together.

When you think of your family, how do you show up? Which role do you play? Are you comfort and care, protection and belief, strength and humor, confidence and a soft place to land? Before the stroke, I was reliable and deep. In this time of my life, I needed to receive. The only thing I could do was rely on each of them to be who they are in life and receive the best from each of them!

The people you choose to surround yourself with can become family. Our friends and co-workers take on different roles in our lives! We have the people we know we can go to at any time for comfort and care. We have the people who will believe in us, even when we can't see it ourselves. We have the people who can make anyone laugh and brighten any room they are in. We have the people who pay attention to details and give what's needed where it's needed.

We also can have the people in our lives who are toxic, causing us to feel drained after spending time with them. We have the takers, people who are all about themselves. If it doesn't work out the best for them, they won't think twice about it. We have the people who are amazing to our faces, but then so hurtful when we're not present.

There are all types of people in our immediate chosen and work families. Each of them is very important. We choose some and others we're given. In each type of family, chosen or given, we can choose how we show up! That is the only thing we have control of.

I know that not every family situation is good. Some are horrible and hurtful. But no matter what family dynamic we are in, it is our responsibility and choice to take care of ourselves and decide how we will interact.

Look for the family members who encourage and support you and your ideas. Those that believe in you and push you to be better than you are by yourself. Who holds a space for you when you may not believe in yourself? I encourage you right now to take time to examine your family, whether they are by blood or by choice.

What role do you play in your family? (Positive or Negative)

Immediate Family:

_____

_____

_____
_____
_____
_____
_____

Chosen Family:

_____
_____
_____
_____
_____
_____
_____

Work Family:

_____
_____
_____
_____
_____
_____
_____

Do you bring life to the people around you? Do you encourage, lift up, and hold a healthy space for them? If your answer is yes, do you have healthy boundaries around who you are and what you give so you don't over give?

_____

_____

If the words you wrote down make you feel like you give everything and don't get anything in return, please hear me. It's time to set some boundaries! What does that feel like? Does it cause a bit of a cringe in your gut? Does it make your face or teeth tighten? Please don't rush through this chapter because this is the biggest foundation in life. No matter what your family life is like, go through these exercises about your role first.

What role would you _like_ to play in your family?

Immediate Family:

_____

_____

_____

_____

_____

_____

_____

Chosen Family:

_____

_____

_____

_____

_____

_____

_____

Work Family:

_____

_____

_____

_____

_____

_____

_____

Is there a gap between the role you currently play and the role you'd like to play? What can *you* do to bridge that gap?

What choices can *you* make to change your reality?

_____

_____

_____

_____

_____

_____

_____

What specific boundaries will you set?

_____

_____

_____

_____

_____

_____

_____

What role does your *family* play in your life? (Positive or Negative)

Immediate Family:

_____

_____

_____

_____

_____

_____

_____

_____

Chosen Family:

_____

_____

_____

_____

_____

_____

_____

Work Family:

_____

_____

_____

_____

_____

_____

_____

What role would you like *them* to play in your life?

Immediate Family:

_____

_____

_____

_____

_____

_____

_____

Chosen Family:

_____

_____

_____

_____

_____

_____

_____

Work Family:

_____

_____

_____

_____

_____

_____

_____

Is there a gap between the role they currently play and the role you'd like them to play? What can *you* do to bridge that gap?

What choices can *you* make to change your reality?

_____

_____

_____

_____

_____

_____

_____

What specific boundaries will you set?

_____

_____

_____

_____

_____

_____

_____

I know that everyone reading this doesn't have the support they want or need. It is extremely important in our personal lives, friendships, family, and business to know WHO we are, what we give, and what we need. When we know those things, it is easier to set boundaries and live the life that has been calling to us to live!

I heard a saying long before my stroke that has stuck with me to this day. You are the average of the five people you spend the most time with. What does that mean? It means that we need to take a look at the people we spend the most time with and decide if it is where we want to stay.

...

How many hours a day do you spend with your work family?

See my example below, then fill in your boxes.

My total work hours in a week are 30.

How many hours do you spend a day with your immediate family?

My total immediate family hours in a week are 39.

How many hours do you spend a day with the family you choose (friends)?

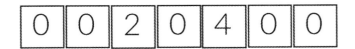

My total chosen family hours in a week are 6.

Now total up the hours you spend which each family.

> 30: Total hours with Work Family (I am self-employed, so I better enjoy time with myself!)

39: Total hours with Immediate Family (I love working from home; that is why this number is high. It wasn't always this way!)

6: Total hours with Chosen Family (I need to work on seeing my chosen family more!!)

Which number is the highest? My Immediate Family

How many hours do you spend a day with your work family?

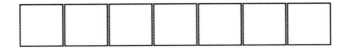

Total hours worked in your week: _____

How many hours do you spend a day with your immediate family?

| | | | | | | |
|---|---|---|---|---|---|---|
| | | | | | | |

Total hours with your immediate family: \_\_\_\_\_

How many hours do you spend a day with the family you choose (friends)?

| | | | | | | |
|---|---|---|---|---|---|---|
| | | | | | | |

Total hours: \_\_\_\_\_

Now total up the hours you spend which each family:

_____ Total hours with Work Family
_____ Total hours with Immediate Family
_____ Total hours with Chosen Family

Which number is the highest? _____

As you look at these numbers, can you see why having a supportive work family is important? Most people spend the majority of their time with their work family.

Who you surround yourself with is everything! I know with 100% certainty that I would not be where I am today without my immediate work and chosen families!

> Tip: When you think, "I can't."
> Instead think, "How can I?"
> Because bridging the gap
> begins with us!

"I can't change this relationship. I can't change my work environment. I can't make them _____!" You're right! You can't! How will you bring life and support and hold a healthy space for someone if the first two words out of your mouth are "I can't"? YOU CAN! What you say is true. Your words have power.

Try it. I dare you! I'd love to know the results. Email me and let me know how your life has changed. (suzy@stroketosuccess.com)

# FIGHT FOR WHAT IS YOURS

Here is a glimpse of what each stage of growth looked like for me. My parents got to experience all these stages with me twice!! At least this time, my terrible twos went by a lot quicker.

> *Newborn*: I couldn't walk or talk. I would sleep all of the time. I was very observant.
>
> *Two-Year-Old*: I was crabby and most things were filled with sass.
>
> *Four-Year-Old*: There was rarely silence. I had a question for everything.
>
> *Eight-Year-Old*: Competitive and excited to learn.
>
> *16-Year-Old*: Hormonal with no boundaries. Very sassy.

There weren't very many "bad" times as I was healing from the stroke. Mostly it was frustration around communication and the lack of it because of aphasia. Aphasia is a communication disorder that affects the brain's ability to use and understand language. Aphasia can interfere with your use of verbal and written communication. Aphasia can also cause problems with your ability to read, write, speak, and listen.

One morning I woke up and felt like I was going to die. It wasn't just a thought, but knowledge. I said to myself, "This is going to happen, and you'll be okay." I had an inner-peace about it. I didn't have the strength or energy to fight for myself. I was tired. Then, pictures of my family ran around my head like a movie. I knew that they wouldn't be okay, especially my brother, so I decided to fight. I decided to stay silent and pray throughout the day! Even though I didn't have it in me for myself, *I knew I had the fight in me for my family.*

I didn't want to be alone that day. I knew I needed to act normal and just get through the day, so I took a shower, got dressed, and went to the kitchen where my dad was making lunch. It felt weird to have wet hair and blow-dry it in the kitchen, but I knew that I needed to be next to someone. I couldn't handle these thoughts on my own, but I didn't want to speak a word about it. I was intentional about fighting to live, for them!

I went to bed early that night and didn't say a word about it. I prayed that when I woke up the thought, or knowledge, would be gone. That I would live a full life with my family! I slept hard that night, woke up slowly, looked around, and thought, "WOO HOO!! I'm still here!" I didn't mention it to anyone right away and have never felt that way again.

There are times in life that you do weird things and have no idea why until you see the reason years later! My brother had been on life saving medication since his twenties, which later caused him to have kidney failure. He was living in Oregon when we went to see his college graduation. It was such a proud time in our family!

After he graduated, my sister stayed with him for a while. Then, they came back to Minnesota. My brother needed a transplant, and Minnesota has some of the best doctors and health systems.

In February of 2011, five months after my stroke, I started working in the infant room at my mom's early learning center. I came home from work and saw my brother lying on the couch. I went over to the couch and lay down on the floor next to him. I put my hand up to hold his, just like he held mine in the hospital.

We talked for a while and I said, "Bro, let's make sure to do this until we get old!"

He said, "Suz, I don't know if I'm going to get old …."

I started choking up and said, "Have I ever told you about blowing my hair dry in the kitchen?"

"No."

So I told him everything about that day and how I was silent. How I decided to fight for him and the family. I told him that I was okay with dying, but I knew they wouldn't be, especially him.

"I fought for you when I couldn't fight for myself. Will you fight for me?" I said. "Anytime you feel like giving up, would you fight for me? Think of the hairdryer in the kitchen."

I realized then that we sometimes need to do things that are out of our normal routine in order to remember things. I will always remember the hairdryer in the kitchen. Now it reminds me to fight for what is mine! That day reminds me to fight for life!

I've been able to share that day with many people. I've had people close to me struggle with addiction, and that story has opened doors to ask if they would fight for me when they can't fight for themselves.

I told my brother that anytime he wasn't feeling like he wanted to fight for himself, or when he was feeling weighed down by it all, to send me a text and I would shoot him a picture of my hairdryer in the kitchen.

So here it is!

Will you fight for what is yours, in life and in your business? Maybe you feel beat up or let down. Maybe you feel tired, like you've tried it all and you're not going to see a change. Think of the people who need what you have, people who are waiting for your products and services right now.

I was talking to a client one day about her direct sales team and said, "If *we* shrink back, *they* will go without." We both paused for a minute to let that sink in!! I had never said that before. When you think of everything that has happened in your life and business, where would you be if the person who introduced you to a thought, product, or business wouldn't have?! What if they didn't connect with you?

I believe that it is our responsibility to offer the gifts, abilities, and knowledge that we've been given, as long as they bring value and provide for a need. That's what I believe that being in sales is, just providing a solution to a need. Nothing more, nothing less. There is no pressure, no defensiveness. If I have the solution to your need, I'm going to work to earn your business. If I don't have the solution, let's be friends!

Seriously!! There is so much freedom in this mindset of sales. It is about the needs of other people and having the confidence to share your product, knowledge, or service with them. You are fighting in business for what is rightfully yours and theirs!!

If we all listen to our gut and step into who we are meant to be, the world would be changed!

Think about that! How many times have you thought of doing something that could change your life and the lives around you, but you have been held back by fear? What would this world look like if we didn't live in fear but fought for the best in each other?

You are here for many reasons. It's not all about being a son, daughter, brother, sister, parent, grandparent, husband, wife, and so on. It's not all about your job, what you do, how many hours you work, or how much money you have or don't have.

I believe you're here to fight for what is yours! To bring life to the people around you. To stand confidently in the gifts that you've been given. To take care of this life you've been given. To share your life! You are here to be in community. No one else can do this life quite like you can! Why not stand confidently in that? Why not live life to the fullest? Why not turn your daydreams into plans with intention? Take purposeful action steps to live in the bonus of your dreams!

What do I mean by living in the bonus of your dreams? Many times when we make a vision board or talk about our goals and dreams, we stop there. Getting to your dream or vision is not the finish line; it's the starting point! The bonus comes when you get to your dream, then the abundance! It will keep multiplying! YES!!! There may be struggles ... after all, I had a stroke. Life is not perfect, but it is worth fighting for what is yours!

What are areas in your life you need to fight for?

_____

_____

_____

_____

_____

_____

How will you fight for what is yours?

_____

_____

_____

_____

_____

_____

_____

Why will you fight for this?

_____

_____

_____

_____

_____

_____

_____

Let's go a little deeper and sit here for a minute. Take a deep breath, plant your feet on the ground, and listen to your heartbeat. Once you read the question below, please close your eyes and put the book down to take time with this. It may feel like a long time, but you'll thank me later. If you need more time, take it!

What are the things you don't want to fight for yourself, but you could fight for someone else? Take your time to really think about this one. If you start to get emotional with this, please let that flow. No good will come from keeping those emotions inside.

_____

_____

_____

_____

_____

_____

_____

_____

_____

Who would you fight for?

_____

_____

_____

_____

_____

_____

_____

I need you to know, *you* are worth the fight!!! If you haven't heard that in a while, or have never heard it, I need to write it again. YOU ARE WORTH THE FIGHT!

What holds you back?

_____

_____

_____

_____

_____

_____

What motivates you?

_____

_____

_____

_____

_____

_____

_____

_____

What action steps can you take today to move forward and fight for what is yours?

_____

_____

_____

_____

_____

_____

_____

_____

Decide what you will fight for and write it here. I WILL FIGHT FOR:

_____

_____

_____

_____

_____

_____

_____

_____

_____

_____

_____

A beautiful thing about fighting for what is yours, whether it is in your personal life, your health, your relationships, or your business, it all starts with YOU! I've heard it said that within 10 seconds of truly deciding something, it is true.

It is how people can think about things for weeks, months, and even years, but when they make that decision – BOOM – it happens or doesn't happen anymore.

I've seen this many times in my life. It's like a light switch with a dimmer. The dimmer can go higher or lower for a long time, but when it's turned on or off, it's done.

If you haven't found strength to fight for yourself, please fight for someone you love! Because you are worth it!

"It all
starts
with me."

*Something that I
remind myself
constantly.*

# SEVEN TO TWELVE TIMES

When learning to talk again, I would practice words in my head. Sometimes I could access the words easily and other times I had to fish for them. It's such a frustrating and interesting process to search for the words you want to say and not be able to say them. When the words come to you, the connection between your brain and mouth doesn't work.

This results in the words not coming out properly. For example, "Happy Bappy," as I mentioned earlier. One thing I used to pride myself on was my memory of people. I have a visual memory, so I would remember a face first and then someone's name. After that, all of the details about how I knew them would come flooding back.

One time I was shoe shopping with my mom at the Mall of America. The girl who helped me looked very familiar. I asked her if she was from the area, but she said no. I asked if she went to a certain church, but she said no. We went through a bunch of different places where we could have known each other. Then, like a lightning bolt, I remembered I knew her when we were younger. I said with a gasp and a ton of excitement, "You're Tiffany Johnson! You had a little white fluffy dog!"

Before I remembered all of the details, I couldn't let the fact that I knew her go. We laughed and she sold me an awesome pair of black stilettos. Knowing people was really important to me. In fact, I prided myself on it. If you asked me to remember life details, such as doing the laundry, they don't stick. But I remember people!

One of the hardest things for me in healing from the stroke was *knowing* that I should know someone, but I just didn't. I loved calling people by name, but that was gone.

Throughout the process, I could repeat things, but coming up with my own words didn't happen as easily. Somewhere in the frustration, I learned that when I tried something six times, I would get it on the seventh time. I don't know when or how I learned this, but I would start to keep track of things and think, "Only a few more times, and I'll get it." In the beginning saying "Mom" was tough. I started out saying "mmmm." Then it changed from "maaa" to "maaa-mmm" to "maa-o-mm" to "ma-omm" to "mommmm" and FINALLY to "Mom" on the seventh time! I don't know why the seventh time worked, but it did. Knowing I got it on the seventh try, I started to try everything seven times.

I am pretty sure that everything I learned as a salesperson helped me to keep trying in the healing of my stroke. It's a joke that I have been in sales since I was a toddler. I would suggest things in a way that would get a yes. I liked to solve problems, especially if it meant that I would get what I was asking for! I remember at a young age trying to figure out ways to make things work, make people happy, and still get what I needed. I learned not to give up and to go after what I wanted.

I am so thankful for my time in sales before the stroke. I got to build a relationship and learn to earn business. There is an art to not taking things personally. I was a telemarketer for a while. Having that job taught me how to brush my shoulders off when people would cuss at me or flush the toilet on me. Yes, they flushed toilets through the phone. Instead of taking this personally, I would laugh to myself. I mean, a grown adult flushing the toilet through the phone was pretty funny. I would just hang up and go on to the next call.

We had to reach out to as many people as possible in three hours. I learned that when I sounded like their best friend on the phone, I made more appointments. That would result in the loan officers closing more deals. I started thinking about each person on the other end of the phone as a person, not just a number.

I've heard many times, "It's a numbers game." To me, however, it was a person game. I remember many families who were struggling with their high interest rate of eight percent or higher; they didn't even know that they were able to lower their interest rate and monthly payments. If I had sounded like just another telemarketer, many families would have been stuck in a financial place where they didn't need to be!! I didn't save anyone's life, but when I thought of the people I talked to as my friends, I got to change a portion of their life, financially and possibly mentally.

Even though many times I thought, "Don't pick up, don't pick up, don't pick up," I'm so thankful that I changed my mindset to "I would love to talk to you and add something of value!"

There is value in what you do! No matter what you do!

I transitioned from the manager of the telemarketing room to a processor because I was great with people and sales. After a few months, I was offered a position as a loan officer. I quickly learned that I enjoyed supporting people and succeeding with them, rather than by myself. Also numbers and I don't get along, so I was a loan officer long enough to get my dad an amazing rate! Haha!

The mortgage company I worked for opened a title company. They asked me to be their account executive. I was excited for the position because I got to design our marketing material, including a glass candy jar with our logo on it. The best part, however, was that I got to connect with people all day. I didn't know anything about the closing process, but I learned very quickly!

As an account executive, I wouldn't stop pursuing my dream client until I connected with them at least twelve times. I read a statistic that 2% of sales close on the first call, 10% of sales close on the fourth call, and 81% of sales close on the sixth call. Unbelievably, 44% of sales reps give up after the first call. Think of the missed business and relationships!

I decided that I wasn't going to be the part of the 44% who gave up after the first call. I would challenge myself to not give up until I connected with my dream client twelve times.

I am usually an all-or-nothing girl and love competing with myself! I also typically don't do something unless it's "pretty." Perfectionism can creep into my thoughts and paralyze me. When I was an account executive, I loved that they gave me the freedom to be myself and create marketing materials that made sense and looked good. They also believed in my idea of making sure we offered something of value. I wasn't just going to go out on "cold calls," but I was going to make "connection calls." There is a huge difference. I wanted to add something of value to the lives of the people I came in contact with, through connection – not just dropping by because I was supposed to.

I learned 3 things very quickly:

#1 – Building a relationship with the person at the front desk is necessary!! I would do this through:

- Making great eye contact.
- Smiling right away after the eye contact was made.
- Introducing myself with a strong handshake and a confident smile.
- Asking them how their day is going – before asking about the decision maker.

#2 – People love receiving a gift.

- I never went on a connection call without something in my hand. The action of giving something to them breaks the ice. Plus, people typically don't turn you down when you have a gift for them.

- Give something that others will enjoy. Maybe something that can sit on their desk with your logo on it. A candy jar with chocolate in it is perfect.

#3 – Confidence and Consistency is KEY!

- Set aside specific sales connection time.
- Set aside a specific time to follow up.
- Set aside time to network & meet new people.
- Set aside time to be creative – to brainstorm – and come up with your Plan of Action for the next week and month.

I don't know many people who enjoy "cold calling." It can be very scary, so feeling anxious about it is pretty normal. Even having a pit in your stomach or having a hard time breathing can happen when some people start to think about "cold calling."

Many people think "what if" when picking up the phone or meeting someone in person. What if:

- I don't know what to say.
- I'm not prepared.

- I stumble with my words.
- I freeze.
- They can tell I'm nervous.
- _____ fill in the blank

Can we pause right here?

WHAT IF?

What is the worst thing that can happen? I'm going to be real and blunt. Will you die? Will you die from picking up the phone or by meeting your potential dream client face to face? (The answer is no – though you may be getting anxious right now even thinking about it.)

Cold calling is just that – COLD! I don't know about you, but I don't like to be cold! I'd rather be wrapped up in a blanket, warm and cozy. To make it about *the connection* with the person you are calling, you will need to change your mindset. This can and will change your feeling about picking up the phone or being face to face.

Maybe you have heard, "It's just a numbers game. Call enough people, and you'll get results." That may be true, but that is not the place I prefer. Yes, if you call 100 people, you will get at least one. But I would rather be intentional about who I talk to and what I say. It is not "a numbers game" but a human game.

When you connect with the person at the front of the office or the receptionist who is answering your phone call, they are like a gatekeeper. Your potential dream client has hired them to weed out the people, conversations, and prospects who would take their time, rather than give something of value.

There is an unseen gate set up in every business. When you connect with the receptionist or *gatekeeper*, you get through the gate quicker.

Here are steps to take to build trust with the gatekeeper:

1.  SMILE. Have a smile on your face no matter what you're doing – on the phone or face to face.
2.  EYE CONTACT. Eye contact is very important! Make sure that you start with both of these! How can you have eye contact

over the phone? Imagine you are speaking face to face – it does wonders!

3. FAVORITES. Find out what their favorite things are – remember them. When you can talk about their favorites or bring them something that they love, they will know that you appreciate them! Not just to get to your potential dream client – but as a person and someone who supports what you need!

Once you have gotten to know him or her, they will look forward to your calls or seeing your face! Your goal is not just to get to know your potential dream client – it is to know their whole support system. Learn how they work!

When you get connected to your potential dream client (the person who will make a decision whether or not they will buy your product or use your services), start this process over!

If you don't feel like you are a "smiley" person – or eye contact is hard for you – don't worry, I've got you covered!

People typically will not turn down chocolate or candy. Crazy, right? I've found that when I walk in with something in my hand and offer it to the person in front of me – it breaks down a defensive barrier – you are giving them a gift. Instead of walking in wanting something – you are giving. This is not the norm. This will set you apart from most people. It breaks the "cold" and encourages the connection. By doing this, it shows the person – the human – that they are not a number. You personally care about them and will work to earn their relationship. That can then turn into earning their business.

Here are three things each of us need:

> To be seen.
> To be heard.
> To be known.

When you show up – on the phone or in person– and do these things, you will be set apart and attract your dream clients.

What does this look like?

The first time I visit an office, I would always connect with the receptionist using a smile, eye contact, and a personal question to make sure they knew I cared about them and their day. Then I would connect with my potential dream client starting the same way. I would also hand them a candy jar with our logo etched on the front of it and say, "I'm Suzy Wigstadt with _____ title company. I would love to get to know you (pause) and earn your business!"

Notice that first and always, I was concerned with the relational part of business. I then would ask them if they had a few minutes.

If it's a YES, I would sit with them and ask them a few questions about their business. Here are examples:

- What is their favorite thing about their job?
- How long have they had this career?
- How long have they been with this company?
- What is their biggest pain point or struggle with their job?
- What is the biggest deciding factor when choosing a title company (your business here) to work with?

If it's a NO, not right now, I would ask if I could schedule a time the following week to stop by and fill up their candy jar. I remind them that I'd like to get to know them and earn their business.

Why would I ask this?

1. Accountability – so I don't chicken out.
2. So they know I'm serious – both about getting to know them and earning their business.
3. Most won't say no to free candy. Even if they think they don't need me, they would say yes to me filling their candy jar!

I wouldn't leave without a date on my calendar – unless they said, "No, don't come back ...."

By the way, that only happened once. I would then ask for their business card, so I could confirm with them before I made the trip the following week. I would also use it for my daily tracking system. When I got back to the office, I put each contact into a spreadsheet to easily find their info and track notes. I tracked everything from our time together to the last time I reached out to them.

Tip: I would ask them if the number and email listed on their card was the best way to reach them. It's something I had to learn the hard way. Sometimes, when I thought I was calling someone's cell phone, it turned out to be their office phone. They were rarely there (or just didn't really want to talk to me ... it happens).

I would leave how I came – with a big smile, eye contact, and firm handshake. I'd tell them, "I can't wait to stop by next week with some candy! I look forward to getting to know you more and earning your business!"

I was in an amazing networking group where one of the members overheard her colleague talking about needing a new title company. Because she knew what I did by listening to me share week after week, she jumped up and told him that he *had* to meet me. She gave me his name and number and said I should reach out to him. We met the following week. He said he'd "be willing" to give us a shot, but I should talk to his senior loan officer. For any lasting change, she would have to be on board.

He walked me over to her office. I gave her a candy jar and introduced myself, "Hi!! I'm Suzy Wigstadt with ___ Title Company! I would love to get to know you and earn your business."

She sat back in her chair, folded her arms, and said, "Good luck."

I was taken back a bit and stood there smiling. She said, "I've been with the same title company for nine years. I'm very loyal, so good luck getting my business!"

Let's pause for a minute here.

What are you feeling as you read this?

_____

_____

_____

_____

What would you do in that situation?

_____

_____

_____

_____

Have you had this happen to you? Where someone flat out shoots you down?

If YES – how did you respond?

_____

_____

_____

_____

_____

_____

Without hesitation (though I felt it inside), I said, "Would you mind if I leave this candy jar here for you and come back to fill it next week? Would the same time and day work?"

She said, "Sure, I guess." (Even though she was a "solid no," she couldn't say no to candy!!)

So I told her that I would see her next week.

I could have curled up in a ball and cried, but I was thankful for her honesty. I look for that in people. I knew she was a dream client and that I would fight for her. I made the decision that I wasn't going to give up until I was their closer.

Guess who showed up with a smile on her face, more candy, and relational questions the next week? THIS GIRL!! I found out her favorite candy was Reece's Peanut Butter Cups and Butterfingers – so I made sure I had those ready for her! I wanted to make sure that she felt cared about and cared for.

Yes, I took extra time with her. To build an amazing relationship, I even brought her lunch before she was our dream client. I stopped by every week … not just three weeks, six weeks, nine weeks. I stopped by twelve weeks in a row. Twelve times!

Earning someone's business is much different than having it handed to you or expecting it! Earning your dream client's business is from your heart – knowing that you both matter and are offering solutions to each other's needs!

On the twelfth visit, she said, "Suzy, do you know how long it's been since my current title company visited me? Outside of closings?"

"No." (I could feel a change in her.)

"It's been three years. You've earned my business!"

Those were the sweetest words I'd heard in the business up until that moment.

Woo-hoo!!

I can tell you there was doubt. There was discouragement. There were times that I wanted to give up, but I kept going to build a relationship with her first! I am so thankful that I took her first words to me as a challenge instead of a defeat! I am so thankful for her honesty. She told me how it was – she didn't skirt around anything – so I didn't either. I met her where she was at that time!

I am now her children's Godmother. I got to go to Australia for a month because of our partnership (She was still closing loans, while I was out of the country. Because she was my dream client, I got paid for them because I brought her business in.) She also helped with information about the debt incurred from the hospital bills. She was an advocate and fought for me!!

Anytime you feel like giving up, KNOW that you are exactly what your world needs!!

I had no idea the friendships that would be built by not giving up! My dream clients became family! Remember the first parallel between healing from the stroke and finding a confident sales voice is that family is everything. They became a chosen part of my family. Though we aren't blood related, they challenge, support, and love me – not just for the financial rewards, but because of who we are.

I received one of the *best* compliments I've ever had from my great friend. She was preparing for an annual pool party. I got there a little early to help and she said, "Suzy, everything is just better when you're around!!"

I've kept that in my back pocket on days that I need it!

If I hadn't stopped by her office twelve times, getting to know her personally, I wouldn't be where I am today! I fought hard for her, and she has fought hard for me!!

# IT ALL STARTS WITH A COOKIE

Living life to the fullest, sharing what you love, and providing a solution to a need is fun!! I love being able to take the anxiety out of things! Most likely, it's because I've struggled with lack of confidence, self-esteem, depression, and anxiety for a major portion of my life!

I have hidden this pretty well from people who saw me from a distance. Many people don't know that you can have a really big smile on your face and feel worthless inside. I believed *everything* for everyone else, except myself.

I came up with a way to live and thrive despite the disconnect between my brain and heart. I learned that when I started and ended something the same way, I didn't have to think about much else because the middle would fill in itself. Talking to people and getting to know them was never the problem. Sharing a solution with them (if I had it) wasn't the problem. It was – how do I build up the confidence in myself to start? Many times, I would just not start.

Oreos (and M&M cookies) are my favorite cookies!! I realized when talking to a client that everything in life starts with a cookie. If we start and end the same, the middle will fill in itself. You wake up and have a routine. You go through your day and have your evening routine. It's amazing that life is like an Oreo cookie and a box of chocolates!

When I started this sales routine, I didn't know where I would trick myself into being confident. When I was offered the job as an account executive, I was excited because that meant I got to talk to people all day!! Woo-hoo!! I am definitely an extrovert and get my energy from people – so I knew that part would be awesome!

But then the battle in my mind started. All of the "what if's" ran through my head daily.

I remember one specific day like it was yesterday. It was a tipping point in my life and career. I was sitting in my car, anxious about going into a connection call. I felt ugly and unprepared. I felt like I wasn't good enough. I felt like everyone could do everything better than I could. I felt unworthy. Why would they say YES to me? The truth is – I was prepared, but I didn't think or feel that I was. The power of our emotions and thoughts is amazing. I wanted to give up. (But that was before the twelve times experience.)

I was so mad at myself! I knew that if my bosses didn't think I could do it, they wouldn't have created the position with me in mind.

So in anger, I turned my rearview mirror toward me and looked myself in the eye. I said,

## "YOU'VE GOT THIS!"

## "YOU'VE GOT THIS!!" I repeated.

## For real! "YOU'VE GOT THIS!"

I started to tear up as anger turned into belief, and belief turned into confidence! Confidence turned into action and action into results! I would never have gone back twelve times without saying that to myself.

It became my routine, my ritual – the top of my sales cookie! I had my traveling office in my trunk, filled with cute and informational marketing folders and candy jars ready to go. If I took time to prepare all of the tools I used for building relationships and sales, why not take the time to build myself up? I mapped out my day to stop by as many offices in a specific area as possible. I would arrive 15 minutes early to make sure that my mindset was in the "You've Got This" space.

Each sales connection day, I would turn my rearview mirror down to look myself in the eye and say, "Suzy, YOU'VE GOT THIS!"

There were times it took me 14 minutes and 59 seconds to believe it, but my feet would not hit the ground until I did! I didn't know it then, but I was intentionally making sure that my mindset was in the right place to attract my dream clients. I needed them as much as they needed me! It would be a win-win-win situation!

When I did this, I got results. New Business. Better Business. Stronger Business!

Can we take a break and talk about Oreos for a second? Have you ever tried the mega stuff? It's too much! Or the Oreo thins, where it's just the cookie, not the filling? It's not enough. I don't even think it's an Oreo. You've got to get the double stuff. It's the best. Not too much and not too little. That is one of the keys to sales.

> *Mega stuff* – you may have great things to say about who you are or what you do, but you come across as a fire hose; you don't let them get in a word. You're telling them all about you – not asking questions and listening. This type of sales OREO just doesn't work.

> *OREO thins* – you may have a great intro, but that's it. You're in and out right away – your dream clients are a numbers game. You were told to do a certain amount in a day, so you get through the day as a salesperson. That type of OREO doesn't work either.

> *Double stuff* – now this is the perfect amount! You've got your intro on the top – you tell them enough about yourself

that you leave them wanting more. You ask thoughtful questions and you listen. You spend enough time with them – but not too much – so they want to see you again. Then you end with setting a date to stop by again!!

It's such a fun, beautiful process, when you have just enough!!

Too many people try to sell without the best stuff – the middle – the personal. When we do that (I have been guilty of this), we are selfishly selling. We care about our needs more than our potential dream client!

Here are some trigger words for me – words that make me cringe in sales and make me feel like it's about the quantity not the quality. There are words that have been around in sales for quite a while. Have you heard them/done them? Do you use them/do them? If you do – no judgment – they just don't sit well with me.

- Numbers game
- Cold Calling
- Elevator Speech

- Reach Out
- Mass Impersonal
- Emailing/Messaging/Texting
- Impersonal Sales Scripts
- Desperate Sales
- Making Your Goals Someone Else's Emergency
- Giving no value when going door to door or on the phone

There are so many "salesy" things that drive me crazy!! Like I said, I've been guilty of it at times and still have to ask myself, "Is that Cold or Connecting?" The beauty in connection is that you are connected with yourself first. It makes such a HUGE difference!

How do you connect to yourself?

_____

_____

_____

_____

_____

_____

_____

Are you currently connecting with your potential dream clients? Or are you *cold* with them?

_____

_____

_____

_____

_____

_____

_____

Do you feel defensive when someone says no?

_____

Do you defend your product or services when they are questioned?

_____

When something doesn't go your way, do you feel resentment?

_____

These are some questions to find out if you are selling through connection or cold selling. (If you'd like more ways to find out if you are cold or connected, visit our website: stroketosuccess.com /cold-or-connected).

My hope is that you don't just *read* the importance of being connected, but that you also *feel* the difference! In my life, I know change has come because I *felt* the *need*. It wouldn't happen if I just thought about it. Change comes when we know it and feel it! So if you find yourself thinking that you have been cold selling, today is a great day to make a change!

You may not love OREOS – but you can use the method in any area of your life! It works to lessen anxiety or get rid of it altogether!

> *Start the Same*: Know your intention and expectations.

> *Let the middle happen*: Get personal – you never know where this will take you.

> *End the Same*: What do they need? What do you need? Know your next step with each other.

# 10 steps for your Sales OREO:

*#1 Prep Yourself* – You can use "You've Got This" if you'd like. It's worked wonders for me!

*#2 SMILE* – Smile at yourself FIRST. It may feel weird, but if you can't smile at yourself, how will you smile at the people in your life?

*#3 Introduce yourself* – Have great eye contact with a strong handshake!

*#4 Give value* – Be intentional in why you are connecting with them.

*#5 Ask about them* – Show honest interest and get on their calendar for the next time you can stop by.

*#6 Keep is short* – Don't take up too much of their time. You will look like you're not busy which may be a red flag to them. Stay long enough to show them you care and will work to earn their business.

*#7 Exit well* – Leave with a smile, firm handshake, and their business card.

#8 *Reply* – "Great to Meet You Today" email.

#9 *Send a note* – Actually send a handwritten card.

#10 *Sales Connection Day* – Stop by their office again within seven days. Same time, same day is best, so they start to expect you.

Start this process over again every time you have a sales connection day. You may need to introduce yourself a few times before they remember you, but building the relationship is worth it!

#11 *BONUS* – Make sure to have a business card with your face on it. It will help your potential dream clients remember you. Or have a digital business card.

How does a cookie apply to healing from the stroke?

While I was in the hospital and couldn't intentionally communicate, I would nod, wink, and smile. When the nurses came in, I would say my name and birth date. The nurses thought that

I was making great progress, but my mom let them know that I had learned what to say to make them happy or leave me alone.

Before I left the hospital, the staff suggested that I go to treatment. They thought that would be the only way that I would fully heal. I didn't have insurance, so that was not an option. My dad dedicated his time to do whatever it took to work with me to heal. He bought preschool books and would spend time with me, quizzing me on my name and teaching me small things.

We had a daily routine. I would wake up, have breakfast, and get wrapped up in four blankets with "Goodness" and "Mercy," the two little lambs my dad bought me. He would read to me and then we would go through preschool books.

I remember sitting at the kitchen table one day. I saw him write something on a sheet of paper and ask me a question. I didn't know what he was asking me, and I didn't know how to communicate with him. I remember feeling blank inside.

As I sit here trying to describe this, I have written and deleted my description about seventeen times!! It is something that is very hard to describe and understand, but I'll do my best.

As I remember this moment, I feel like I was looking down at the table watching him write. I picture my dad writing $1 + 1 =$ on a sheet of paper and looking at me.

As I play through this in my mind, I want to tell him "two," but my mindset was one of a newborn, so I didn't know the answer or even understand the question. It's so interesting to me. I've lived in a place where all I knew was body language, tone of voice, and eye contact. I felt things deeper. I knew things without understanding words.

In healing from my stroke, I learned a routine; we started the day the same and ended it the same. As I got stronger and grew in my ability to speak, the middle of my day was filled with people who loved me and would challenge me in growth.

One example was a family friend who dropped off amazing food and sat with me on the couch going through a photo album. She showed me a picture of her and "this guy." I asked who it was. She said it was her husband. I giggled and said, "You're not married!"

She then showed me pictures of two cute kids. I asked her about them. Not only were they her kids, but she said that I actually took the pictures of them. I laughed and told her she was lying!! I didn't believe her. I knew her by her maiden name and without kids.

As I relearned everything and connected to the past through memories, I had a process. I would listen a lot and sit with their words. I would search for the meaning in what they were saying. There were times when the memory would turn on like a light bulb, quick and bright. I could remember everything right away. There were other times where a memory would come back to me like a lottery card.

As people would talk and tell me things, it was like I was scratching off the silver stuff. It would take a bit longer, but once the card was fully scratched off, the whole memory would return! I learned not to give up and to be patient with myself.

The brain amazes me. Connection between the people we love amazes me! I am so thankful that my family started the same and ended the same with me daily! It included belief, love, patience, and tenacity!! They would do whatever it took to *get me back!*

"Suzy, everything is
just better when
you're around!!"

*I've kept that in
my back pocket on days
that I need it!*

# LEAVE YOUR JUNK AT THE DOOR

I had mostly amazing doctors and nurses while I was in the hospital. I say mostly because there was this one ....

I was so uncomfortable when she was in the room. She was a specialist. I can't recall which field, but I can go back to the moment very easily! I was in the bathroom and overheard her say something. I don't remember her words, but I remember how it made me feel like she didn't have my best interest in mind. I could feel that she had something else going on and brought it into my room with her.

I got a stomachache and tensed up when she was around. At that point, I couldn't communicate my feelings. Once I could talk, the memory affected me so much that I had to tell people about it. I shared it with my mom, but she didn't notice anything different about the nurse. In fact, we still disagree about it to this day! I wonder if that is normal between a patient and their caretaker? There are memories that line up with each other where reality and the state I was in are the same. Then there are memories where I was in a dreamlike state. I would come in and out of reality.

Some of my "chosen family" stayed with me during the day in the hospital. I lived with an amazing family for three years. The mom in the family became the big sister who I never had. The family visited me a few times. I had a great connection with their sweet daughter, whose nickname was "Baby Girl." She was a toddler at the time. She had a favorite type of blanket. She wouldn't go anywhere without one. I think she had about 10 of them – one or two were always in the wash. They were precious to her. When she visited me in the hospital, she gave me one of her blankets and a green bracelet. As I write this, I am getting choked up because I remember her leaning in to give me the bracelet and blanket. I wanted to talk so badly. I wanted everyone to know that I was okay and would be okay.

The night she gave me the bracelet, I had a dream about it. It was actually half reality and half dreamlike state. My mom slept over at the hospital each night with me. The dream was so real to me!!

I was in a room that looked like a control room of a movie theater. The movie showed kids who were hungry all over the world. I was able to go feed and take care of them, but I had to make a sacrifice. I had to squeeze feet first into something that looked like a pillowcase; then I would go through the projector and into the film roll to become a part of the movie.

Because this was so real, I had to do something to let my family know that I would be okay. They shouldn't worry about me. I was going to help people. I knew that I needed to give my mom my green bracelet. That's how she would know that I would be okay. I woke her up in the middle of the night to give it to her. She kept giving it back to me, saying that it was special and mine. She said I should keep it, but I insisted until she finally accepted it. We both went back to sleep.

I didn't notice the green bracelet until about a month later. She was wearing it. I pointed to it and started crying. The hospital memories flooded through my head and I said, "Wait – that was real?"

She said, "Yes! It was. It was very real!"

We took a moment to talk about how far I had come. We compared stories of our experience. That's where we noticed our different reality with *the one* nurse.

I felt safe with everyone else who came into my hospital room. Different people brought out different things in me. My brother, sister, bonus big sister, and auntie brought comfort. My parents brought strength. My cousin, who is a doctor, brought smiles. A baby that I had just taken his eight-month photo shoot brought communication and joy. An old co-worker got me to laugh and eat. I didn't know specifically who each person was, but I knew how I felt with them and what they drew out in me. This *one nurse* drew out anxiety and discomfort.

The only thing I can think of is that she had issues that she was carrying in her own life and didn't leave them at the door. I was in a very vulnerable place. I felt whatever she was carrying was real. This memory of my time in the hospital is important for me to share. I'm thankful that I can talk about it – because many people may not be able to remember, communicate, or describe what they went through. I'm not saying that everyone goes through this, but I want to bring awareness to how we can affect people and not even know it.

It has impacted me so much and has a huge parallel to my life and the people in my world!! I would love to encourage you to leave your problems at the door when you are going from place to place. I don't mean "keep it in" – NO. If there are things that you're feeling personally, let the people in your life know. Reach out to receive help. There is nothing wrong with honesty and receiving!

What I mean by leaving your problems at the door is to make sure that you check your mindset. Check your heart. When you go out of your home for the day, are you ready for the day? When you come home from your day, are you ready for your home life? Taking a few minutes to yourself is good and healthy!! Make sure that your stuff doesn't affect the people around you, especially if you're in a caretaking or sales position.

It is easy to just go through our day and think of our own issues. It is easy not to reach out or let people in. Life can be frustrating and draining, so why spread that to the people in your life?

If you carry junk around with you, what does it look like, feel like, sound like?

_____

_____

_____

_____

_____

_____

_____

What are a few areas you can improve on with your mindset?

_____

_____

_____

_____

_____

_____

How do you encourage the people in your life?

_____

_____

_____

_____

_____

_____

_____

What is a victory in your life today?

_____

_____

_____

_____

_____

_____

_____

_____

_____

# "You've Got This!!"

*Repeat as many times as needed.*

# LISTEN TO YOUR GUT

As adults, I feel like we have lost a childlike faith that believes something if you say it. We've gained a cynical view of needed proof of security before we act. We've lost an excitement about what could be. We don't sleep when we feel sick. We don't make time for the things we enjoy. We've learned to compare ourselves and the need to keep up with the status quo, instead of creating our own normal. We've learned to not listen to our gut. We tend to go until we break. To work hard and not necessarily smart. We've been taught to ignore that still small voice, to dismiss the passion that is calling out to us, sometimes even screaming to us to listen.

Why do we shut off that still small voice? Why do we ignore the things that we once loved? My dad has always said that he admires my faith like a child. You say that something is going to happen and I believe it!!

There have been points in my life where I've lost that. But when I am fully myself, that belief is still so strong. There is no other way to be for me! There is no room for doubt. I've been called an eternal optimist and gladly accept that title. I dream big and wide! Not just for myself, but for everyone around me! I don't know how to be any other way!! It is why I surround myself with people who are action-oriented. It is why I love "my rock" – my person. My parents talk about how everyone is either a rock or a balloon. I always thought that I was the rock because I don't like small talk. I always go deep. I want to know the depth of you, not just the surface. I've learned that I'm definitely a balloon. When I met my rock, I knew in my gut that I needed him! I knew he was it!

I knew it in my gut, my heart, my mind! A rock grounds the balloon so that they don't fly away. A balloon brings movement to the rock, so they don't stay in the same spot. When two rocks are together – they don't go anywhere. When two balloons are together – they just fly away. You can have a light rock or a heavy balloon. He's the light rock to my heavy balloon!

I am so glad that I listened to my gut and gave him my number the first day that I met him! The second year anniversary of my stroke came 11 days after we met. I told him that I wanted to write a book. He gave me a gift that day. It was a notebook, colored pens, silly putty, a whoopee cushion, and a card saying that he believed in me and supported me in writing my book!

It was one of the most meaningful gifts I've received. He saw me, heard me, and knew me! Though we hadn't known each other for a long time, he gave me exactly what I needed. A notebook to start, colored pens to make it pretty and color coded, silly putty for a writing break, a whoopee cushion for a good laugh and to make the weight of my story a little lighter, and his card – he reached into my soul with his supportive words!!

Getting a second chance at life, going through the growth period from the mindset of a newborn to a 28-year-old adult, I got to relive the innocence of being a child. I learned how to trust my gut again!

I wonder where we lose our innocence. Where do we learn not to trust our gut? Where do we learn that we need to be people pleasers? Where do we learn that how someone else feels matters more than what we feel? Where do we learn to snuff our dreams, to not believe that they will come true? Where do we learn to think that we're not enough? I know that everyone doesn't feel this way.

I am not pointing blame, but sharing my curiosity. I would love to bring up the conversation because I believe too many children grow up with these beliefs and turn into adults with these beliefs.

You are enough!

How does reading that make you feel? I have cried many tears in disbelief. Not believing that I was enough. Wherever trust in your gut was taken away, I pray that you're able to go back to that place and get it back. Believe that you are enough!

I didn't listen to my gut when it literally told my body to slow down. I learned to medicate. I learned to ignore. I learned to cover up. I learned to push aside. My body told me for at least three months that I needed to take care of myself. I didn't pay attention when it told me to stop, so my body stopped itself.

If my life can help someone listen faster, all of this was worth it! I've learned so much from the stroke and healing that I wouldn't want anything different. But I would not wish it on anyone else because of the things my family went through.

If your body is telling you something, please listen!! Our bodies are meant to work. What we dream about is meant to happen. We have so many opportunities to be healthy and reach our dreams. Determine in yourself to take action. Listen to your heart and your gut, and I promise you won't be disappointed!

What has your gut been saying?

_____

_____

_____

_____

_____

_____

Have you been ignoring it? If yes, why?

_____

_____

_____

_____

_____

What one step will you make to take action and listen to your gut?

_____

_____

_____

_____

_____

_____

I've found something so interesting in the healing process. Kids are like sponges. They soak up everything that we say and don't say. They watch and listen and learn from it all. I have been a babysitter or nanny for over half of my life. It's so interesting to me that as adults we teach our kids not to get into a car with a stranger, and yet we have Uber.

As a photographer, I saw that all the time! I would tell the parents in a family shoot – don't stress about our photo shoot – your kids will feel it and react!! I would tell them that it was my job as their photographer to earn their trust and reactions. When they smile, amazing! When they're sassy, amazing! I would love to capture the stage they are at and the stage your family is at! Know that the shoot will be great – and I'll capture beautiful moments that you don't even realize.

I was a road manager for eighteen months; it was one of the best times of my life. I learned and grew so much! One of the things I saw was a family who made "their normal." It wasn't like anyone else's, but it was theirs. I remember how they taught their kids how important they were. They would be in the spotlight naturally, but their family unit was the most important thing!

When a parent was talking to someone and one of the kids needed something, they would put their hand on the parent's shoulder and wait. They didn't interrupt over and over, but they waited.

The parent would say (to the adult they were talking to), "Excuse me for a second." Then they'd say to the child, "Yes honey, what do you need?"

How amazing is that! They learned great communication and importance. The kids learned that they were important and that the adult's conversation was important!

I also learned about the difference between being polite and trusting your gut with strangers. I remember one time I was in a crowd with one of the kids. A man came up to us and was very much in our faces. Being polite, I said "Hi."

After saying "hi" to us, he started asking the boy questions. There was no response. He then started saying that the child was shy, almost in a taunting way.

So I got Mama Bear-ish and said, "No, Sir. He is polite and has been taught not to talk to strangers. And, Sir, you are that!! So he is doing exactly what he should be doing!! Have a nice day."

Then we left, as I trusted his gut feeling and physical reaction to that guy. Instead of playing into what the adult was saying, I saw his reaction and acted on it.

In going through the process of healing and caring for kids during many years of my life, I believe it is so important to teach our kids to be mindful – to say please and thank you, to open doors, to help others when they can, and to be kind. I also believe in teaching them to be mindful of themselves. What are they comfortable with and what are they not? We are the adults and should listen to that. We are the responsible ones to teach the next generation.

Think of the kids in your life. We haven't met our kids yet, but we're excited to someday. We do, however, have bonus kids who are important to us, so I will think about them.

Think about what they are learning from you. This is not a judgmental moment!! This is a time to evaluate. No one is perfect! Perfectionism = Paralyzation. Please don't let PERFECT be the goal – but being real, being solid. Always trying. Never giving up. You are exactly what the children in your life need!!

"Perfectionism

=

Paralyzation!!"

*Don't let perfect
be your goal.*

# YOU ARE EXACTLY WHAT YOUR WORLD NEEDS

I am a sales girl. Not only am I "in sales," but I love a sale!! I will search and search for the perfect thing to not pay full price for!! It totally seems like a funny way to start this parallel – between healing and sales, but it will make sense.

This drive to get the most for my money started with my babysitting money. I learned that if I waited to the end of a season when the stores needed to make room on the floor for the next season, I could get an item for 75-80% off. So I would wait. My best friend would always have the newest things at the beginning of the season. It was an ongoing joke about how much we both paid for the same item. "Of course, I paid $65 for that short-sleeved button up jean shirt, and you got it for $6," she would say!! It was fun (for me)!!

After my stroke, the love for a deal showed up when I went shopping for the first time with my sister. We decided that I would only spend $10. I went to the back of the store where the clearance items were and found so much that I wanted. She kept telling me no, that I couldn't get it all. I had to stick to my budget. I found this super obnoxious black shirt with bright red glitter lips. It was $9.95 with no tax on clothes in Minnesota – so it was perfect for my budget. She said, "Are you *sure* this is what you want?"

I was, and I was excited! We had a great time together, out of the house! At that point in my healing I would quickly become exhausted and get headaches. When we got home, I said something sassy. She looked at me and said, "My sister is back!!"

Tears were streaming down our faces – the ugly cry kind. She was exactly what I needed in that moment! That was exactly what I needed to hear! I think it was exactly what she needed, to know that her big sister was coming back!!

There are so many stories that I could tell you in the healing from my stroke. Like how my brother stayed in Minnesota until Christmas to make sure that I was taken care of and to be with family. Like my mom staying overnight at the hospital, only leaving my side if someone else was able to be with me. Like my dad getting me the "Goodness and Mercy" stuffed lambs to communicate with me in my current stage and as a reminder that I was being taken care of. Goodness and Mercy now sit in my office as a constant reminder that no matter what, I'm held.

Here are a few specific stories of the people in my life being EXACTLY what I needed.

After the stroke, I was on prescribed medication. One of the side effects was that it could cause thoughts of suicide. My family didn't tell me the side effects because they've thought I'm a hypochondriac (I don't think so – I just feel everything deeply).

There was a point where I got pretty down. I didn't have much energy and just wanted to sleep. I was planning to learn how to drive again with my dad one day, but it snowed about six inches the night before. I don't enjoy driving in the snow when I'm healthy, so to learn in it was totally out of the question for me! I told him I didn't want to go out in the snow. He said he would take that time and make me my favorite stew.

At that time, I had healed enough to be alone for a few hours. My bonus sister would pick me up later that afternoon, a few hours after my dad left for work.

My dad and I hugged goodbye, and I went upstairs to eat. I had been curled up on the couch all day. I opened the fridge and thought, "You don't want to be here anymore."

I was surprised at the thought!! It was almost an outside voice. I looked at the counter where there was a butcher's knife laying there. I thought, "Nope, that's not how you would do it, you would ...."

I didn't let myself fill in the silence! I didn't finish that sentence. I knew I needed to get out of the kitchen, away from the knife. I slammed the fridge door shut, grabbed some stew, crackers, and a Sprite, and sprinted downstairs! I knew I needed something in my belly – something salty and something sweet.

My dad making the stew that day was exactly what I needed. If the stew wasn't made, I would have been in the kitchen longer.

My bonus sister came to pick me up. I told her right away what had happened. She was taking me to my mom's early learning center for a program that night and said I needed to tell my mom and family everything!!

My mom took me to my doctor the next day. She fit me into a 15-minute slot – which led to over an hour with her. We made a plan to wean me off of the medication.

Everyone in my life stepped up to fill my many needs!! My uncle connected me to an amazing chiropractor who I saw multiple times throughout the week. When I first went to his office, I wasn't able to speak. My family had to interpret what I was trying to say and tell the story for me. I remember being in his office trying to say words. I would get frustrated and look at my brother, sister, mom, or dad to fill in the blanks!! They were exactly what I needed!! I believe without that chiropractic care, I wouldn't be where I am today!

What are ways in your life someone has been exactly what you've needed?

_____

_____

_____

_____

_____

_____

How have you been exactly what someone needed?

_____

_____

_____

_____

_____

_____

After my stroke, I shared that I got to work in an infant room as an assistant teacher. It was amazing for three years. At about two and a half years in, I got the itch to start selling again. I loved the opportunity and honor to grow with the families and babies in the infant room, but I knew that I was supposed to get back into sales.

My brother had really good advice and said, "If you don't do it now ... then when? You'll never do it."

He was right!! I was scared. What if's filled my thoughts. I knew that I was good at sharing the love of jewelry before – so I thought about it for two months. I didn't tell anyone about it. I knew I could probably make it happen, but I didn't want to make or force anything. I wanted it to just be! It would be proof to me that I was supposed to do it. In one day, I was contacted by three people asking me if I was sharing the love still. I was a bit blown away, but then said to myself, "If I can book six parties – I'll do it!"

Guess what happened? I booked seven! Isn't it crazy when you put your mind to doing something, how many times you can surprise yourself!!

I then decided I would step into photography full-time with a bit of jewelry on the side. I was excited to draw out confidence in women through jewelry and capture beautiful moments that would never be duplicated but remembered for a lifetime through photography!! I was solid in this decision; I was going to work for myself.

A sales position opened up for a website design company. I was offered the position for a few months, but I didn't know if I wanted to work for someone else again or if I wanted to continue to work for myself.

After negotiations and being able to continue with my photography, I decided to take the job! That position in sales brought my confidence back. I got to do what I was designed to do again! I was able to mentor the sales team, bring in 19 new clients, and build amazing relationships.

After six months I was wrongfully fired. I was completely shocked. I was the leader in sales and building relationships. I had just had my best month. It took me a while to shake that because my integrity was questioned, but I've come to realize that I wouldn't be where I am today without that unexpected push. Even though I didn't know it or feel it then, it was exactly what I needed.

That led to the next person who was exactly what I needed! Right after I accepted the job at the website company, I was asked if I'd like to be the sales and marketing director for a title company that a great friend of mine owns. I was honored at the offer and would have loved to work with her right away, but I had just committed to being an account executive. She told me, "If anything changes ... you let me know!"

I took that to heart. As I was being fired, her face and her words kept running through my mind, "If anything changes, you let me know." I was in disbelief, but then almost laughing, I thought, "Okay, the best is on its way!"

I called my friend a couple hours after I was wrongfully fired and said, "Is that position still available?"

Her reaction was exactly what I needed to hear! She yelled into the phone with excitement, "YES!! When can you come in and talk about it? We've been searching for six months, but no one has felt right."

Are you kidding me right now?

She was what I needed! She believes in me. She supports me. She saw my gifts, abilities, shortcomings, areas for growth, and worth. She invested in me and I got to invest in her company. I got to build relationships and set up Value Building Classes for realtors and loan officers. It was like I was home! She and her team became family! I know I've said this a lot throughout this book, but I'm going to say it again. I wouldn't be where I am today without her!! *Again* – family is everything!

I was just recently hanging out with an old friend I used to babysit for; she has known me since I was sixteen. She introduced me to a friend of hers. My old friend asked me to share my story with her friend (my new friend). I shared a lot of what I've shared here with you. She asked, "Suzy, are you the same person as you were before the stroke?"

I took some time to think about it and said, "I'm not 100% sure. I feel the same, but I also know the ins and outs of my day and get frustrated at times when my memory isn't what I'd like it to be

… or when I feel like I should know something. I should be more, do more, and remember more … so I'm not sure!"

My friend said, "You are the same Suzy, just stronger!"

WOW!

Tears started rolling down my face, because that was exactly what I needed to hear! I needed to have that nugget in my back pocket to take out on certain days when I'm not feeling it.

She didn't even know the gift she was giving me!! There is something so beautiful about giving and being *exactly* what someone needs. Many times you don't even know what you've given them or the impact you will have in their lives!

When we give what is needed, the world is changed!!

Here are the things I believe we need to do to *be exactly* what someone needs:

- Follow our heart.
- Listen to our gut.
- Step out and up with confidence.
- Lead with intention.

That's it. It's so much better to give than to receive! And how cool is it that when we give, we also receive so much!! Isn't that crazy awesome?

It gets me so excited to bring that fact to people. It's so much better to give! In everything we do – life and business! That is one of the ways I get to daily Bring Life and Speak Life!

I get to draw out the inner confidence in entrepreneurs and sales teams to find their confident sales voice, offer out of the box sales solutions, personal sales training, and accountability in action.

I am thrilled for each day in my life that has brought me to today. The good times along with the bad, hard, easy, ugly, and beautiful times! They all have shaped me!

I've got one more place to pause to sit with a few questions.

What is something you need right now?

_____

_____

_____

_____

_____

_____

Who is a person to connect with right now who could provide *exactly* what you need?

_____

_____

_____

_____

_____

Where could you use a boost in your confidence?

_____

_____

_____

_____

_____

_____

Who needs *exactly* who you are and/or what you do?

_____

_____

_____

_____

_____

What are five things you will take action on today to be *exactly* what the people around you need, including yourself?

1: _____

2: _____

3: _____

4: _____

5: _____

When you take time to invest in yourself and listen to the still small voice or feeling that is calling to you, your life will be changed. A bonus that comes along with that is the world around you will also be changed!

# POSSIBLE ACTION STEPS

If you would like a FREE digital workbook that goes deeper into the action steps this book lays out – please email Brian@stroketosuccess.com with the subject line: FREE Digital Workbook.

If you would like to know more about our Personal Sales Training and Accountability, please visit our website – stroketosuccess.com to set up a FREE 15-minute sales consultation.

If you would like to hire Stroke to Success to speak at a conference, retreat, or team meeting, please contact Brian@stroketosuccess.com.

THANK YOU for your love and support! Thank you for reading this book cover to cover! It would be an honor to work with you – if that is what your gut is telling you!

Make it a great day and invest in yourself to live the life that is calling to you to live!

And if you feel someone needs the message in this book, please share it with them.

www.stroketosuccess.com